KT-572-687

A1080495

Books in the Linkers series

Homes discovered through Art & Technology
Homes discovered through Geography
Homes discovered through History
Homes discovered through Science

Myself discovered through Art & Technology
Myself discovered through Geography
Myself discovered through History
Myself discovered through Science

Toys discovered through Art & Technology
Toys discovered through Geography
Toys discovered through History
Toys discovered through Science

Water discovered through Art & Technology
Water discovered through Geography
Water discovered through History
Water discovered through Science

First published 1996 A&C Black (Publishers) Limited
35 Bedford Row, London WC1R 4JH

ISBN 0-7136-4373-0
A CIP catalogue record for this book is available from the British Library.

Some of the people featured in this book are models.
Commissioned photographs by Zul Mukhida. Design by Jean Wheeler

Consultants: Grant Jones, Art Adviser, E. Sussex
Ian Punter, Adviser in Design Technology, E. Sussex

The publishers would like to thank the children in Reception, Year 1 and Year 2 of
Wallands County Primary School, Lewes, who worked so hard to produce the artwork featured
in this book, and Judy Grahame and Annette Bolton who facilitated and guided its production.

Acknowledgements

Associated Press/Topham; 16 (left), Bridgeman Art Library; Galleria degli Uffizi, Florence 10 (left),
Museo Colleo, Venice 10 (right), Chapel Studios; 4 (left), 8 (left), 14 (left), 20 (left), Positive Images; 12 (left), 15
(right), Topham Picture Point; 22 (left), WPL; 18 (left), Zefa; 6 (left).

Printed and bound in Italy by L.E.G.O.

Myself

discovered through
Art and Technology

Karen Bryant-Mole

Contents

Me 2

Colourful me 4

Material me 6

In and out 8

Self-portraits 10

Body prints 12

Body painting 14

Clothes 16

On the move 18

The future 20

Happy or sad? 22

Glossary 24

Index 24

A & C Black • London

Me

This is a photograph of a girl called Zara. You probably have photographs of yourself, too.

When you show them to other people you might say, 'That's me!'

But there is much more to you than just one photograph can show.

'Me' is not only what you look like.
It's the things you like to do, what your
memories are, what your favourite food is,
who your friends are and much, much more.

'Me' can change. Your age changes
every year. Last year Zara was six.
This year she is seven.

Your body changes,
your feelings change and
your interests change, too.

In this book, you will find ways
to explore 'me' through art,
design and technology.

Colourful me

When Mukesh looks in the mirror he sees a boy with brown hair, brown eyes and a patterned shirt.

Why don't you have a look in a mirror and paint what you see?

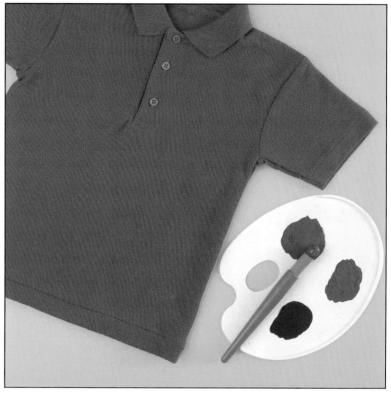

Sometimes the colours in your paintpots aren't exactly the right shades.
You can change colours by mixing different paints together.

Make a painting of yourself, trying to match all
of the colours as closely as possible.

Material me

Unlike photographs, bodies and clothes do not feel smooth all over.

The boy in this photograph is having his hair cut.
What does it feel like when you run your fingers through your own hair?

You could make a picture of yourself by collecting together some materials and choosing the ones that look or feel like you.

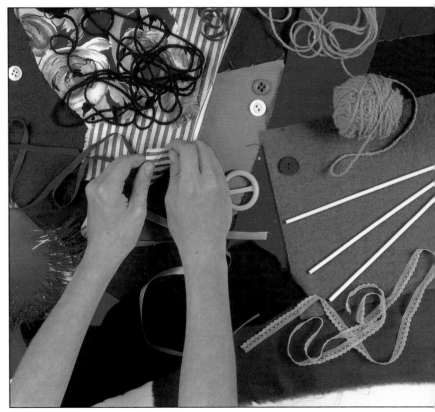

Pictures made from fabric and
other materials stuck onto paper
are called collages.
They look good and are also
interesting to touch.

In and out

This photograph shows some children playing.

Paintings and photographs are flat. But children are not flat, they have bits that stick out and bits that go in.
You could make a model to show how you go in and out.

You will need to use a material that can change shape.
You should be able to push, pull, squeeze, pinch and poke the material.
Clay or play dough would be good materials to use.

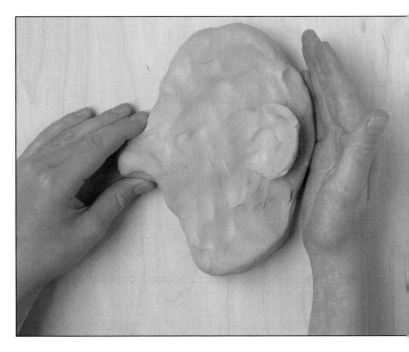

Squash a piece of clay or dough onto a board.

Then, use your fingers to shape the clay or dough into a model that looks like your own face.

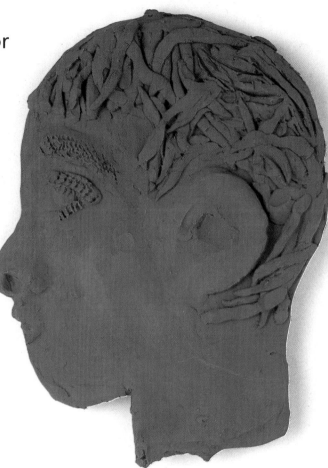

This sort of model is called a relief sculpture.

9

Self-portraits

Things that people make or paint to look like themselves are called self-portraits.

This painting is a self-portrait by an artist called Raphael.
It was painted by Raphael nearly five hundred years ago.
He used oil paints on a special material called canvas.

This sculpture is a self-portrait, too. Antonio Canova carved it from marble about two hundred years ago.

This self-portrait is a photograph.

Salima Ahmed stood in front of the camera, holding a lead that was connected to the camera. When she pressed a button on the end of the lead, the camera took the picture.

You may be able to find some more pictures of self-portraits in books about artists.

11

Body prints

Can you see the foot prints
in the sand?
They were made by people
as they walked along
the beach.

You can use paint to make prints on paper.
Use a sponge to cover the underside of your
hand in paint, then press your hand onto
a sheet of paper.

Remember to wash your hand afterwards!

Why not make foot prints, finger prints,
toe prints or even elbow prints?

All of these designs have been made using body prints.

Body painting

The Australian aborigine in this photograph has decorated his body with a special type of paint.

Around the world, different peoples paint their faces and bodies in different ways and for different reasons.

You could use face paints like these to decorate your face.

You can make up a pattern or you could try to make your face look like a cat or a clown.

What is this boy pretending to be?

Clothes

As fashions change, new clothes are designed and made.

There are lots of reasons why we wear clothes. We wear them to keep warm or to keep cool and because they look good.

Clothes can be made from different types of material.
You could try making clothes from paper. You might need some tools for cutting and joining.
Be careful! Some tools are sharp.

What do you think of these hats?
They are cheap to make but
would not be much
use in the rain.

Can you think of any
other good points
or problems about
wearing these hats?

On the move

This boy's body moves and bends when he does gymnastics.

We can move because we have joints.

Some joints are a bit like hinges. They join two parts of the body and let the parts move.

One way of showing this is to make a card puppet with joints. There are many different ways to fasten the pieces together.

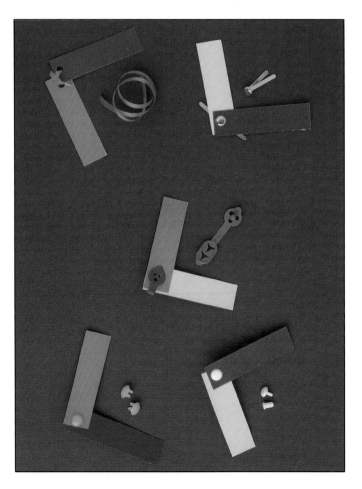

Here are some 'me' puppets.
Can you see the joints?

The future

Have you seen pictures of yourself as a baby?

Everything that has happened to you since your birth is called your past. Everything that is yet to happen is called your future.

Why not make a picture showing what you might like to do in the future?

Here are some of the different drawing tools you might use to make your picture. Different tools produce different results.

Lois-Hannah thinks she might like to be a nurse.

David wants to be a racing driver.

Happy or sad?

Our faces can show how we feel.
Our faces change as our
feelings change.

A simple way to make a mask is to use
a paper plate as a base.
Ask a grown-up to help you cut out
eye holes and a nose flap.
Do not stick anything sharp through
the plate when it is in front of your face.

You could make a set of masks to
show how your feelings change.

The children who made these masks have taped clean lolly sticks to the backs so that they can hold them in front of their faces.

What feelings do you think these masks show?

Glossary

aborigine a native Australian

clay a type of earth that can be used to make pottery objects

design pattern or picture

memories places, people and times from the past

sculpture a type of art that is not flat, often made from clay, stone, wood or metal

shades differences in a colour, for example, light blue and dark blue

tools a hand-held object, often used for making things

Index

bodies 3, 6, 18
body painting 14–15
body prints 12–13

clay 8, 9
clothes 6, 16–17
collages 7
colours 4–5

designs 13

face painting 14, 15
feelings 3, 22–23

friends 3
future 20–21

hair 6
hats 17

joints 18

marble 10
masks 22–23
materials 6–7, 8, 10, 16
models 8, 9
moving 18–19

paintings 8, 10
paints 4, 10, 12, 14
paper 16
photographs 2, 8, 11
play dough 8, 9
puppets 18–19

relief sculpture 9

self-portraits 10–11

How to use this book

Each book in this series takes a familiar topic or theme and focuses on one area of the curriculum: science, art and technology, geography or history. The books are intended as starting points, illustrating some of the many different angles from which a topic can be studied. They should act as springboards for further investigation, activity or information seeking.

The following list of books may prove useful.

Further books to read

Series	Title	Author	Publisher
	Face Painting	J. Russon	Wayland
Artists' Workshop	Portraits	C. Roundhill & P. King	A&C Black
First Arts and Crafts	Collage	Sue Stocks	Wayland
	Masks	"	
	Painting	"	
	Printing	"	
	Puppets	"	
First Skills	Starting Painting	S. Mayes	Usbsorne
Get Set Go!	Collage	Ruth Thomson	Watts
	Drawing	"	
	Painting	"	
	Printing	"	
How To Make	Face Painting	C. Caudron & C. Childs	Usborne
	Masks	R. Gibson	
Knowhow Books	Puppets	V. Philpott & M.J. McNeil	Usborne
What Shall I Do Today?	What Shall I Draw?	R. Gibson	Usborne
	What Shall I Paint?	"	
You and Your Child	Paint Fun	R. Gibson	Usborne